Last Frontiers For Ma

# Working with the
# OCEANS

## Lawrence Williams
## and
## Alan Collinson

## Evans Brothers Limited

# CONTENTS

# INTRODUCTION

This book is about the oceans of the world. Oceans are difficult and dangerous places for people. We can stay below the surface for only a short time. On the surface we struggle to survive the power of an ocean in a severe storm.

At the present time we understand just a little about the edges and surface of the oceans. We understand almost nothing about the depths. We are only just beginning to explore this frontier and the opportunities it might give us.

Oceans are full of life. But even as we begin to understand this life we are also in danger of destroying it. We are dumping our poisons into the oceans and pretending that this does not create problems. We are taking out fish far faster than they can breed and replace themselves. We are in danger of treating the oceans as badly as we are treating the jungles. We are behaving in the oceans as we are at all our frontiers. We are not respecting the environment.

The dangers of this crisis are clear but, fortunately, so are the opportunities. Because the oceans are so large we may not have harmed them very much so far. There may still be time to develop a partnership with the life of the oceans. We can still save the oceans from our own greed and ignorance.

**Waking up a shark.** This tiger shark has been tagged with an electronic marker so that its movements can be traced. To do this the biologist had to make the shark unconscious. He is trying to wake it up by shaking it and making it swim. If he fails the shark will die. Studying marine life is helping us to understand the oceans.

# CHAPTER ONE

# THE OCEAN BASINS

## WATER AND LIFE

The water that fills the ocean basins and covers 71 per cent of the Earth's surface makes our planet unique in the Solar System. Without the special properties of water life would not be possible on Earth. Our planet itself would also be completely different.

About 3.5 billion years ago some very primitive plants living on the Earth developed a green-coloured substance called **chlorophyll**. A major group of plants that did this is named **phytoplankton**. These tiny plants float in the oceans.

Plants with chlorophyll were able to develop new processes on which all modern life depends. They were able to use the energy of sunlight to take hydrogen out of the water.

**This led to two life-giving processes:**

1 The energy of **hydrogen** was combined in the plants with the gas carbon dioxide. This produced simple sugars and starches as forms of energy. This process is named **photosynthesis.** It happens in modern plants in much the same way as it did in primitive plants all those millions of years ago. Plant life depends on this process.

2 The **oxygen** released from water by the primitive phytoplankton began to collect in the atmosphere. At the same time the amount of carbon dioxide gradually lessened. As a result the kind of air we have today was slowly produced. It is partly the activity of the phytoplankton in the oceans today which keeps the balance of gases in our atmosphere.

**These two processes are responsible for life as we know it today: not just life in the oceans but all life on our planet.**

**The Mother Ship.** This ship is engaged in research in the ocean. It is named the mother ship because other smaller craft are operated from her. At the stern can be seen a deep water submersible craft being prepared for launching. On board are laboratories and other equipment for the scientists who work in her.

Water has special properties of its own that help to keep the oceans and the atmosphere in their present condition.

1 At just above freezing point water expands instead of contracts. This means that ice is slightly lighter than water. Ice floats instead of sinks. If it sank, ice would gradually collect in the bottom of the Polar Seas turning them into solid ice. There would be no chance of it melting in summer. Ice would fill the ocean basins as far as the temperate zones and the Earth would have a permanent Ice Age.

2 Water has a huge capacity to absorb heat. (See chapter 2.) So the oceans in the hot parts of the world absorb heat and then carry it to cooler areas. This warms the air and the land of the temperate latitudes. (See the map on page 12.)

3 Water has the ability to dissolve almost anything. Once dissolved the substances tend to be held apart by the water. They do not join up to form new chemicals. This means that plants like phytoplankton can get all the chemicals they need for growth directly out of the ocean. They do not need roots. Even seaweeds have no true roots.

Some of the dissolved chemicals in the oceans are very useful. The best known is common salt (sodium chloride). Salt can be extracted from seawater by building small enclosures called pans. These pans are flooded either at high tide or by the people letting seawater in through a gap. The pan is closed and the water evaporates leaving the salt behind.

In some areas farmers have come to value seaweed as a rich fertilizer for their lands. They collect it from beaches and spread it on the fields. In Norway and Scotland the large seaweed named kelp is harvested for its minerals on an industrial scale.

In some arid countries, such as Saudi Arabia and Israel, seawater is being used in two ways. Salt for cooking and other uses is being extracted from the water. The purified water is also being used for crop irrigation. The huge factories where this happens are named desalination plants.

When we say that water is essential for life we mean that in more than one way.

## Key words

**chlorophyll** – the green pigment (colouring material) in plants which enables them to use sunlight to separate oxygen and hydrogen in water.
**environment** – what a place is like. People can change an environment by caring for it or by misusing it.
**evaporate** – to turn a liquid into a gas. In this case the hot sun evaporates the water leaving salt behind.
**latitude** – the distance of a place from the Equator. This is usually measured in degrees. For example, the Tropic of Capricorn is 23½° South. (See the map on page 6.)
**photosynthesis** – the process in green plants of making food by using sunlight.
**phytoplankton** – very small plants, usually single-celled, which float and drift in the oceans.
**primitive** – very simple.
**temperate zones** – the parts of the world between the cold polar zones and the hot tropical lands, where temperatures are generally more moderate.

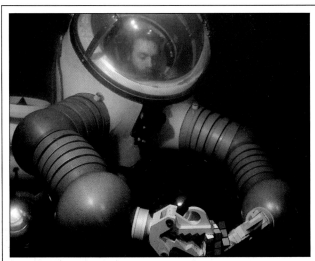

**One man submersible craft.** The operator of the submersible is showing how well the artificial hands can be used for difficult tasks. Although this submersible can be operated at depths of several hundred metres it could not survive the enormous water pressures in the deeper ocean.

## OCEANS, SEAS AND CONTINENTAL SHELF

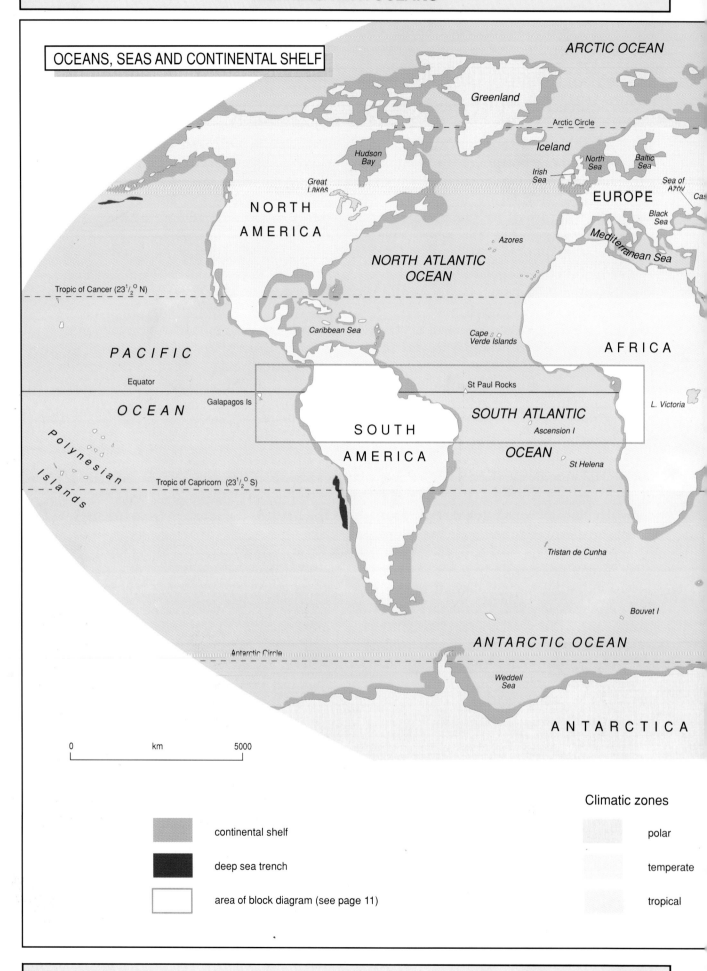

ARCTIC OCEAN

Greenland

Arctic Circle

Iceland

Hudson Bay

North Sea

Baltic Sea

Irish Sea

Sea of Azov

EUROPE

Cas

Black Sea

Great Lakes

NORTH AMERICA

NORTH ATLANTIC OCEAN

Mediterranean Sea

Azores

AFRICA

Tropic of Cancer (23$\frac{1}{2}$° N)

Caribbean Sea

Cape Verde Islands

PACIFIC

Equator

St Paul Rocks

OCEAN

Galapagos Is

SOUTH ATLANTIC

L. Victoria

Polynesian Islands

SOUTH

AMERICA

OCEAN

Ascension I

St Helena

Tropic of Capricorn (23$\frac{1}{2}$° S)

Tristan de Cunha

Bouvet I

ANTARCTIC OCEAN

Antarctic Circle

Weddell Sea

ANTARCTICA

0    km    5000

Climatic zones

continental shelf

polar

deep sea trench

temperate

area of block diagram (see page 11)

tropical

## LOCATION OF OCEANS AND SEAS

A map like the one on this page is **flat**, and because the surface of the Earth is **curved** it cannot give a true picture of how much of the surface of our planet is covered by water. For example, the Pacific Ocean covers nearly one third of the whole surface of the globe. It is twice the size of the Atlantic. It contains more than twice the amount of water because some of it is much deeper than the Atlantic. The Antarctic Ocean is also difficult to show on this map.

Most of the names of the oceans and seas were decided by early European navigators, explorers and map-makers. The name 'sea' was also used for large, inland areas of water where there was no river flowing out to another sea. The Caspian Sea is an example. Large inland areas of water such as the Great Lakes of North America or Lake Victoria in Africa which have rivers flowing out of them are not named seas.

The map also shows the shallowest sea areas and the deepest sea areas. The shallow areas are named the continental shelves because they are the submerged edges of the continents. The very deepest areas are all deep, narrow trenches. The floors of the oceans between these shallowest and deepest waters are not smooth surfaces. They are broken by many ridges and chains of sea mountains. Often there are volcanoes on them. Some ridges come to the sea surface as islands. A line of such islands from Iceland to Bouvet Island is shown on the map on this page. All these are peaks on the mid-Atlantic Ridge. In this map the climate zones are shown only on land areas. This is because so much detail is given in the oceans.

A S I A

Sea of Japan

PACIFIC OCEAN

East China Sea

bian ea

Bay of Bengal

South China Sea

The Maldives

helle Is

NDIAN OCEAN

A U S T R A L I A

| | |
|---|---|
| *OCEAN* | a great body of water occupying a major part of the Earth's surface |
| *Sea* | a body of water close to or surrounded by land - sometimes confused with ocean and used interchangeably |

1. Find out what is meant by a **map projection**.
2. How are some land areas affected by the projection used on this map?

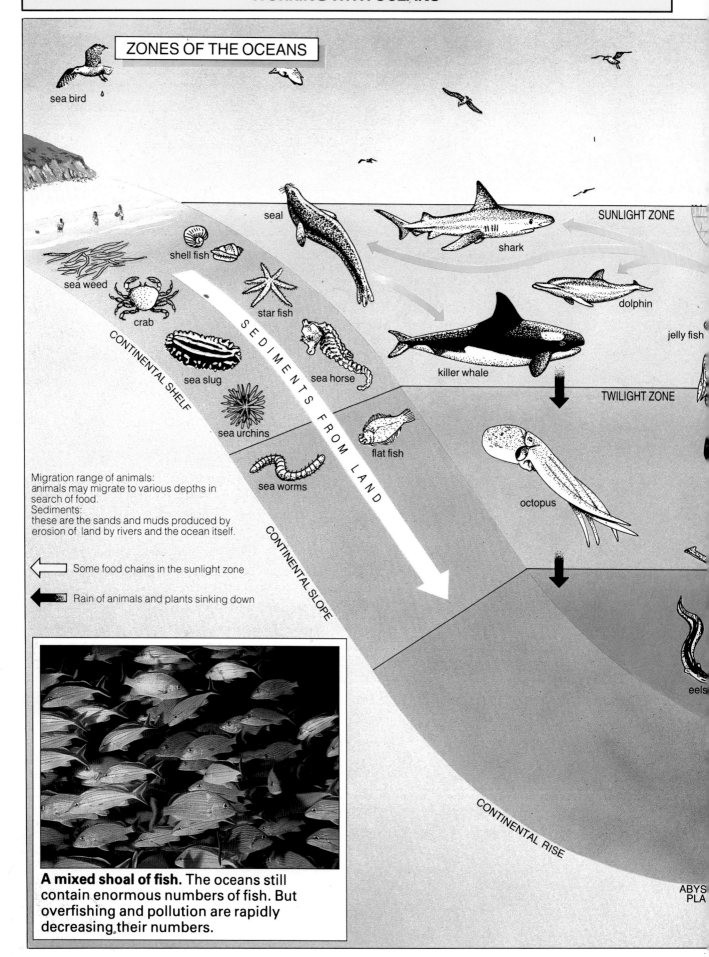

## ZONES OF THE OCEANS

sea bird

SUNLIGHT ZONE

seal

shark

shell fish

dolphin

sea weed

jelly fish

crab

star fish

CONTINENTAL SHELF

SEDIMENTS FROM LAND

sea slug

sea horse

killer whale

TWILIGHT ZONE

sea urchins

flat fish

octopus

Migration range of animals:
animals may migrate to various depths in
search of food.
Sediments:
these are the sands and muds produced by
erosion of land by rivers and the ocean itself.

sea worms

CONTINENTAL SLOPE

Some food chains in the sunlight zone

Rain of animals and plants sinking down

eels

CONTINENTAL RISE

ABYS
PLA

**A mixed shoal of fish.** The oceans still contain enormous numbers of fish. But overfishing and pollution are rapidly decreasing their numbers.

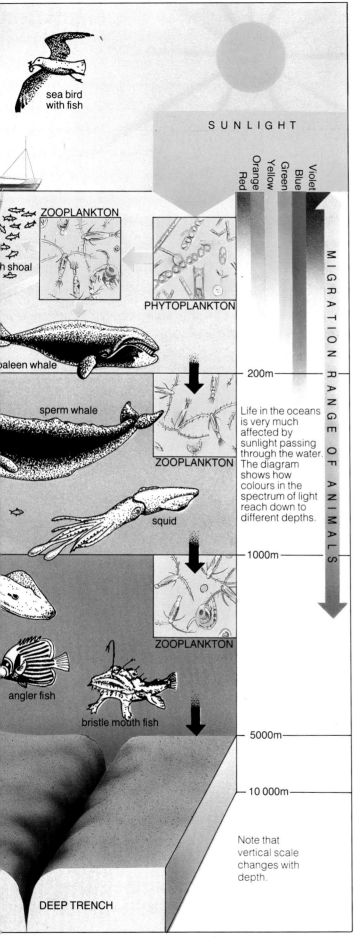

sea bird with fish

SUNLIGHT

Violet
Blue
Green
Yellow
Orange
Red

ZOOPLANKTON

h shoal

PHYTOPLANKTON

baleen whale

sperm whale

ZOOPLANKTON

squid

MIGRATION RANGE OF ANIMALS

200m

Life in the oceans is very much affected by sunlight passing through the water. The diagram shows how colours in the spectrum of light reach down to different depths.

1000m

ZOOPLANKTON

angler fish

bristle mouth fish

5000m

10 000m

Note that vertical scale changes with depth.

DEEP TRENCH

# BELOW THE SURFACE OF THE OCEANS

The depths of the oceans can be divided into zones. This is shown in the diagram.

In the upper zone live the phytoplankton. They are eaten by very tiny floating animals named zooplankton. In turn these are the food for fish and other marine creatures. Then these fish are caught and eaten by larger carnivorous (flesh-eating) fish, seals, seabirds, dolphins and some whales. This passing of food from plants to animals to other animals is named a **food chain.**

In the twilight zone there is not enough light to support the growth of phytoplankton. Most of the animals here rely on a rain of plants and animals sinking down from the lighted zone above for their food. In the deepest and darkest zone of all, many of the fish have light organs to find and attract prey to their jaws (see the photograph on page 38).

Each of the ocean zones relates to a part of the side of the ocean basin itself. This is clearly shown in the diagram. For example, the continental shelf relates to the twilight zone.

Not shown in the diagram are other divisions in the water. There are layers at different temperatures and salt concentrations. The water in these layers may be moving in different directions.

**Key words**

**abyssal plain** – the deep ocean floor beyond the continental slope.
**continental shelf** – the submerged outer edge of the continental plain.
**continental slope** – the gentle slope at the margin of the continent.
**food chain** – movement of food from plants which trap sunlight to animals which feed on them and are in turn fed on by other animals.
**zooplankton** – a variety of tiny animals which float and drift in the oceans.

## THE CHANGING SHAPES OF THE BASINS

In the early 17th century, Sir Francis Bacon pointed out that the east coast of South America and the west coast of Africa could be fitted together. He suggested they might once have been joined. Today we know he was right, but it has taken the technology of the last 50 years to prove it.

We have discovered that the Earth's skin is made up of immensely strong **crustal plates.** The **continents** are made of lighter rocks and sit on top of them. The plates move very slowly as the molten rock beneath them moves. This molten rock is named **magma.**

The diagram on page 11 shows the structure of the Atlantic Ocean Basin between tropical South America and Africa. The middle of the ocean floor is cracked and magma is building up the mid-Atlantic Ridge. At the same time currents in the magma are flowing away from the ridge and dragging the cooled rocks of the crustal plates with them. As these two huge plates move apart so South America and Africa are moved apart. The Atlantic Ocean is becoming wider.

When the magma bursts out into the Atlantic Ocean it is cooled immediately and forms the rocks we call lavas. (See the photograph below.) In this way the volcanic islands of the mid-Atlantic Ridge are being built up. On the map on page 6 you can work out the position of the ridge by imagining a line joining up the islands such as St Paul Rocks and Ascension Island.

Although the outpourings of lava may be violent and rapid the movement of the plates themselves is very slow. South America and Africa are drifting apart at the rate of a few centimetres a year. This gradual movement of the continents is named **continental drift**.

Where plates are drifting apart, as in the Atlantic Ocean, the ocean basins are being enlarged. Chains of islands are built up as a central ridge. The edges of the basin are marked by a continental slope which is sloping very gently.

Where plates are drifting together a different situation may develop. This can be seen in the left-hand side of the diagram on page 11. Here the plate on which South America lies is moving west and colliding with the plate of the south-east Pacific Ocean. In this case most of the volcanic activity is on the land area of the Andes

**Surtsey Island on the mid-Atlantic Ridge.** Surtsey Island is a volcano forming an island on the mid-Atlantic Ridge. Lava can be seen spilling into the sea. Huge clouds of steam are formed as the lava is cooled to form solid rock. With every eruption the island becomes larger. It is being built up in our lifetime. Surtsey is marked on the map on page 6.

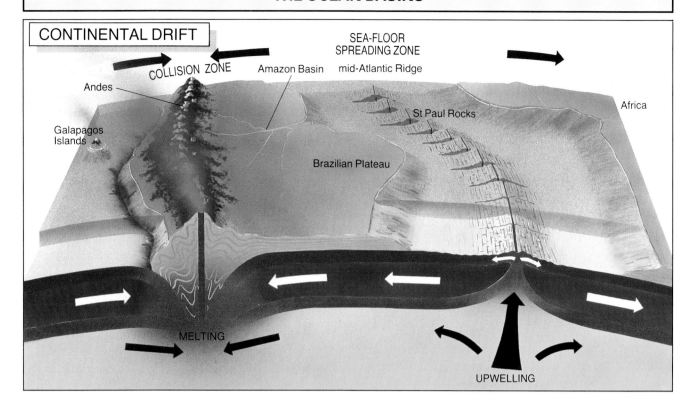

CONTINENTAL DRIFT

SEA-FLOOR SPREADING ZONE

COLLISION ZONE    Amazon Basin    mid-Atlantic Ridge

Andes

St Paul Rocks

Africa

Galapagos Islands

Brazilian Plateau

MELTING

UPWELLING

Mountains. The other rocks of the Andes have been strongly folded by the slow but amazingly powerful collision of the plates.

The effect on the changing shape of the ocean basin is quite different from the Atlantic. The Pacific Ocean Basin is actually deeper close to land than far out in the ocean. Also the continental slope is much steeper here than on the east side of South America.

Another feature of the ocean basins affected by continental drift is their capacity or how much water they can hold. This capacity has been increasing over millions of years. As a result sea level has been falling in that time. If the shapes of the basins now changed so they could hold less water, the sea level would begin to rise again. (Some other reasons why sea levels may change are discussed on pages 25 and 40.)

Continental drift has one other important effect on the oceans. The slow movement of the plates is not a steady movement. Two plates may come into a collision zone and enormous pressure builds up between them. For a long time this pressure may not be released, but eventually the rocks will break under the stress. This is very sudden. The breaks we name faults, the shock waves we name earthquakes.

Earthquakes can be very destructive on land. But if they occur on or close to the edge of an ocean basin they can set up huge ocean waves which the Japanese name 'tsunamis'. (Wrongly named 'tidal waves' in English.) These waves travel across the ocean about 160km (100 miles) apart, and at speeds up to 725km (450 miles) per hour. They are extremely destructive to shipping when they strike the coast. There is now a network of advanced warning stations for them all round the Pacific Ocean.

**Key words**

**crustal plate** – a rigid section of crustal rock.
**continent** – land mass of rocks lighter than the crustal plate on which it sits.
**continental drift** – the slow movement of the continents as they are carried by the crustal plates.
**magma** – intensely hot molten (liquid) material from the interior of the Earth. When it reaches the surface it cools to form rocks. If cooling is very rapid the rocks are named volcanic rocks.

# CHAPTER TWO

# CURRENTS, WAVES AND TIDES

## OCEAN CURRENTS

The map shows the world pattern of ocean currents. Near the Equator the flows tend to be parallel to the lines of latitude. Outside the tropical areas the main flows are from west to east and from lower to higher latitudes. For example, in the north Atlantic, the Gulf Stream and North Atlantic Drift move from the Caribbean Sea north and east towards northern Europe. Currents which run from lower to higher latitudes are warm currents, for example the Gulf Stream. Those which run from higher to lower latitudes are cold, for example the California Current.

Ocean currents are not like rivers. They are very broad drifts of water moving at only about 8–10km (5–6 miles) each day. However, some currents are much faster than this. For example, the Gulf Stream and the Kuroshio current reach speeds of be-

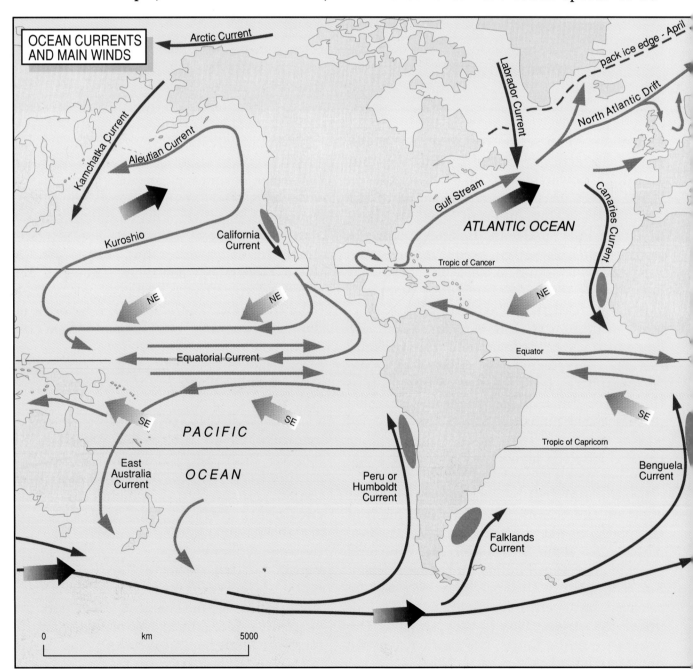

OCEAN CURRENTS
AND MAIN WINDS

Arctic Current

Kamchatka Current

Aleutian Current

Kuroshio

California Current

NE

NE

Equatorial Current

SE

PACIFIC

SE

East Australia Current

OCEAN

Labrador Current

pack ice edge – April

North Atlantic Drift

Gulf Stream

ATLANTIC OCEAN

Canaries Current

Tropic of Cancer

NE

Equator

SE

Tropic of Capricorn

Benguela Current

Peru or Humboldt Current

Falklands Current

0        km        5000

tween 90 – 160km (60 – 100 miles) each day.

Most of the ocean currents are driven by the winds that blow across the surface of the sea, dragging the water with them. As a result there is a close connection between ocean currents and world climates. The warm currents carry huge quantities of heat to higher latitudes. For example, **every square centimetre** of the surface of the Kuroshio current gives up to the air **each day** as much heat as a person would generate if they ran continuously for an hour.

If ocean currents did not carry heat away from the Equator that belt of the Earth's surface would be unbearably hot. At the same time the temperate zones would probably be too cold for people to live there.

The movement of warm water away from the Equator is balanced by cold water flowing in the opposite direction as cold currents. The map shows this quite clearly. There is a circulation of water which prevents it piling up in one place. The general world sea level is maintained.

Inside this general circulation of ocean waters there are a number of smaller local circulations as well. One of the most important of these involves some of the cold currents moving towards the Equator. Strong winds named Trade Winds push these currents **away** from the land. To replace them deeper water has to move **inshore and upwards.** As this deep water wells up to the surface it brings with it large amounts of dissolved salts and minerals which plants can use for food. These waters are therefore very rich in phytoplankton, zooplankton and fish. This is enormously important for the people living on these coasts. They need a good source of food from the sea because many of the lands the cold currents flow past are deserts or semi-deserts. For example, the Canaries current lies off the coast of the North African Sahara, the Benguela current lies off the coast of the Kalahari desert and the Peru current lies off the coast of the Atacama desert (see map above).

There are some other important divisions in the waters which the map cannot show. For example, there are layers of water above and below each other which are at different temperatures and salt concentrations. The water in these different layers may be moving in different directions, in some cases opposite to each other. Scientists believe that some of these differences could be used to generate electric power.

These different layers often get mixed together at the edges of the oceans. They may also be mixed by vertical swirls (vortices). Little is known about these vortices. They were only discovered in the last 20 years by astronauts observing the Earth from a United States' Space station.

INDIAN OCEAN

seasonal current reversal

Agulhas Current

West Australia Current

| | westerlies | | warm current |
| | trade winds | | cold current |
| SE | south-east | | up-welling water |
| NE | north-east | | |

The map on page 12 shows the surface circulation of ocean currents. This is a result of the circulation of winds which cause the currents. In turn the currents affect the world's climates by moving heat from the Equator to the tropics. Then a second system moves heat from the tropics towards the poles. **The systems of currents and winds and climates all interlock.**

However, these systems do not operate quite as smoothly as might be expected. Just as the effects of continental drift include the violent events of earthquakes and tsunamis, so there are violent events connected to the circulation of ocean currents.

One of these events is shown in the photograph and diagrams on these pages. **Hurricanes** are extremely powerful and destructive but they begin from something altogether quieter and slower.

The water which crosses the oceans from east to west in low latitudes becomes very warm on its slow journey. This heat passes to the air and can set off rising columns of air as violent thunderstorms. If these are particularly strong and join together the rising columns of air develop into hurricanes. (Also named typhoons or tropical revolving storms.) The diagram on page 15 shows the structure of one of these. There is a huge spiral of swirling air round a calm centre which is named the **eye** (see weather map on page 15). This is also clearly shown in the photograph taken from Space.

People who live in the tracks of hurricanes know how destructive they are (see right-hand photograph on page 25). Only occasionally, as in England in October 1987, do other parts of the world experience winds of the same force. In tropical areas which frequently have hurricanes many larger buildings are specially reinforced. An early warning system operates like the one for tsunamis. Oceans are dangerous places to be during a hurricane.

In spite of the damage at sea level, hurricanes do have an important function. The eye is one of the main ways in which air from the stratosphere is mixed with the air of the lower atmosphere. At the same time high-level polluting dusts from aircraft and volcanic eruptions are extracted and brought down to the ocean.

A less violent event that disturbs the environment happens when the ocean currents do not maintain a smooth circulation. An example occurs in the eastern Pacific Ocean. Sometimes so much warm water collects in the western side of the ocean that it spills back to the east. This warm water covers over the cold current that flows along the coast of Peru. At the same time sea level may rise by as much as a metre. This is named El Niño (the child) by local people because it often happens at Christmas.

This change from cold surface water to warm surface water upsets the weather pat-

**Hurricane Elens, 2 September 1985.** This photograph was taken from the Space shuttle Discovery. The picture shows the great swirl of air round the calm eye at the centre. The pattern in the clouds is very clear. The hurricane is about 190km (150 miles) across. The eye is about 28km (15 miles) across. It is through the eye that air from the upper atmosphere (the stratosphere) is being drawn down to sea level.

## HOW A HURRICANE WORKS

STRATOSPHERE

up to 16km (10 miles)

| | track of hurricane |
| --- | --- |
| | spiral of warm air rising and cooling |
| | cooling air currents |
| | cool air sinking |

This hurricane is also shown in the map below

terns of the **southern hemispere**. It is not just Peru that is affected. It has happened seven times since 1960 and has caused droughts in India, Australia and South America.

### Key words

**eye** – calm centre of a hurricane.
**hurricane** – a violent rotating tropical storm.
**isobar** – a line on a map passing through places of the same atmospheric pressure at sea level (iso = equal; bar = a measure of air pressure). The average pressure of the air at sea level is about 1000 millibars (1 bar).
**southern hemisphere** – the half of the world south of the Equator.
**vortex (vortices)** – a whirling motion of air forming a hole in the centre named the eye.

## WEATHER MAP OF THE HURRICANE APPROACHING LAND

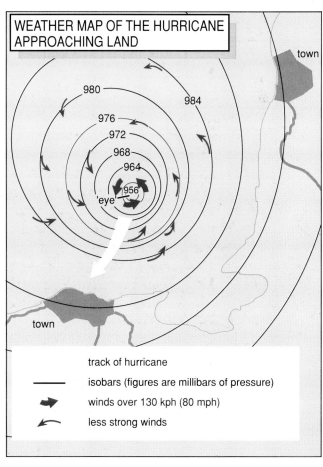

town

980
984
976
972
968
964
'eye' 956

town

| | track of hurricane |
| --- | --- |
| | isobars (figures are millibars of pressure) |
| | winds over 130 kph (80 mph) |
| | less strong winds |

# WAVES

The winds that drive the world's ocean currents also make waves. Waves are the result of friction between the faster moving air and the water (see diagram A). Local winds have the same kind of effects but on a local scale. For example, the western coasts of Europe do not always have their winds and waves brought from the southwest by the prevailing southwesterly winds. Local storms can produce waves from the north instead.

It is the currents that move great masses of water, not the waves. In the open sea the wave shapes travel forward but the water in the waves does not. The particles of water move in circles but stay more or less in the same place. Diagram B shows the movement of water particles inside a wave. At depth this movement dies out. A submarine can pass deep below a storm and the crew will not experience any wave movement at all.

In conditions of strong winds two changes take place in the waves. Firstly, the depth to which the water is disturbed increases. Secondly, the wave tops, named the crests, may topple over as the wind drives them (shown in diagram A). We see this very clearly as the toppling wave crests make 'white horses' or 'white caps' on the sea. (See large cover photograph.)

Waves carry with them the energy of the wind. This energy wears away or builds up the coastline. Where strong waves break against rocky coasts their power breaks the rocks, carves out cliffs, caves, arches, stacks and **blow holes**. The cliffs are worn back and a rocky platform is left in front of them. This is an example of **erosion** by the sea. (See the photographs on pages 24 and 25.)

Where waves break on beaches they push sand up the beach and comb it down again as the water runs back to the sea. If the waves break on the beach at an angle they not only move sand up and down the beach but also along it. This sideways movement is named **longshore drift** (see diagram C). When this process is very active, and there is a gap in the beach such as a river mouth, then a spit of sand or gravel might develop. An ex-

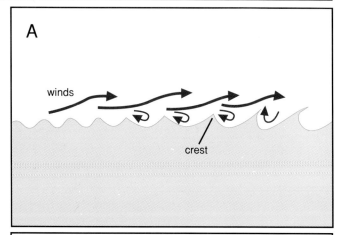

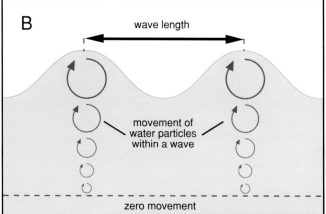

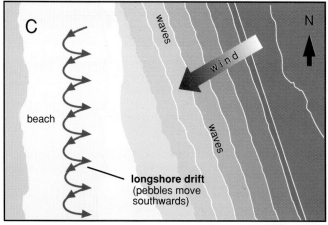

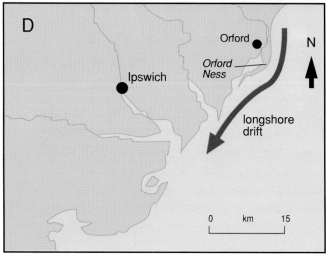

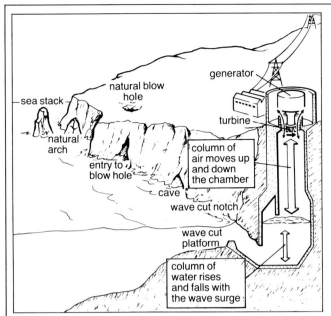

**A Norwegian design for using wave power.**
In the centre of the diagram is a natural blow hole. This is the result of erosion by the sea along a weakness in the cliff. On the right is the artificial blow hole developed to produce electricity from the wave surge into and out of the blow hole.

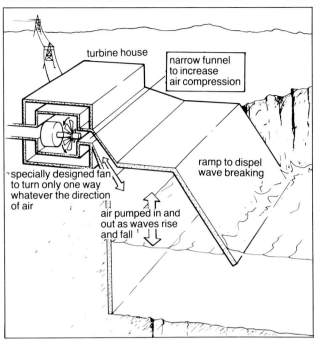

**A British wave power design is being tested in Scotland.** It is hoped that this design will be built into new port breakwaters in southern India. These will help to protect the ports and also generate electric power.

ample is Orford Ness (diagram D on page 16). Orford was once a flourishing port but has been cut off by the spit. This is an example of **deposition** by the sea.

Ways of harnessing the enormous energy of waves have been neglected. Our energy needs are met by burning different kinds of fuels such as wood, coal and oil. These sources of fuel are becoming exhausted. We have also discovered that burning these fuels damages the environment (see chapter 5). As a result scientists are investigating ways of using the huge amounts of energy available in the oceans.

Two modern schemes for extracting power from waves are shown on this page. The Norwegian scheme uses an artificial blow hole to force air past a turbine at the top of the cliffs. The British scheme, being developed in Scotland, uses the waves to generate compressed air to turn the turbine. Both schemes use turbine blades which always turn the shaft in the **same direction**. It does not matter whether the air is being pushed past as the wave surges in, or drawn back as the wave sinks back.

## Key words

**blow hole** – a tunnel punched from a cave to the land surface above the cliffs by waves and compressed air.

**deposition** – the laying down of solid material (sand, mud, lime etc.) by a natural agency (wind, running water, the sea).

**erosion** – the breakdown and removal of rocks. For example, rocks being broken down to sand grains and then carried away by the sea.

**friction** – a dragging force made by two surfaces in contact when one or both of them are moving. For example, waves dragging on the sea bed.

**longshore drift** – the shifting of sand and pebbles along the shoreline by waves breaking at an angle to the beach.

**prevailing winds** – the winds that blow most often, e.g. in most of Great Britain the prevailing winds are southwesterly winds.

# TIDES

The reasons why tides occur are shown in the diagram and boxed text on page 19.

In the past this constant movement of water was regarded as a nuisance. Ships could only enter and leave harbour when the tide was right. Port authorities had to spend great amounts of money building docks so ships could remain afloat while the tide was out. Only a few great harbours, such as Southampton and New York, have estuaries that make dock construction unnecessary. This is because the shape of the nearby coasts causes the **tidal range** to be very small.

The major reasons why tides are important have only been understood in the last 100 years.

Firstly all the plants and animals which live in the **coastal wetlands** depend on tides for survival. The ebb and flow of water over beaches, in and out of estuaries, across marshes and mangrove swamps, keeps them alive. The incoming tide brings fresh supplies of food and oxygen. The outgoing tide carries away waste products and excess mud, and also helps keep the river mouths clear.

Secondly we now recognize that tides represent a huge and reliable source of energy. In this case, unlike winds and waves, it is not solar energy but **gravitational potential energy**. In the past this movement has been used to turn small tide mills which were rather like ordinary water mills on rivers. But today engineers see a much bigger potential than that.

In France, at St Malo on the River Rance, engineers have constructed a barrage (dam) across the estuary. In the lower part of the barrage, turbines have been fitted. When the water flows through the turbine tunnels as the tide rises and falls, the turbines are turned. They are linked to generators and electric power is produced. In Great Britain serious attention is now being given to building a similar tidal power station across the River Severn estuary. If the final studies are successful, construction could begin before the year 2000. In Canada, a tidal power barrage similar to the one at St Malo, has already been constructed in the Bay of Fundy.

**High tide and low tide at Alma, Bay of Fundy, Canada.** These two photographs show that the tidal range is very great here. In 1983, a tidal power barrage began to produce electricity in this bay using the enormous potential energy of the tidal range. Tidal range is the difference in height between highest and lowest tides. In the open ocean it is only 1–3 metres. Near coasts it can be very great. For example, in the Bay of Fundy it is 14–15 metres (44 feet). At St Malo it is 13½ metres (40 feet) and at London Bridge 7–8 metres (21–24 feet).

## THE EARTH, THE MOON AND THE TIDES

Gravity is the force given out by any mass of material. As you are reading these words, the ground beneath you is being moved very slightly up or down by the pull of the Moon's gravity. We call these pulls the **tides** and the diagram on the right shows how they work. The strong pull of the Moon draws up the water into a bulge towards it.

On the opposite side of the Earth at the same time the Moon's pull is weaker so the spin of the Earth throws the water of the ocean into another bulge. As the Earth turns right round in 24 hours, each part of the ocean will be pulled into bulges twice, as graph A shows. These are called **semi-diurnal** (half-day) tides.

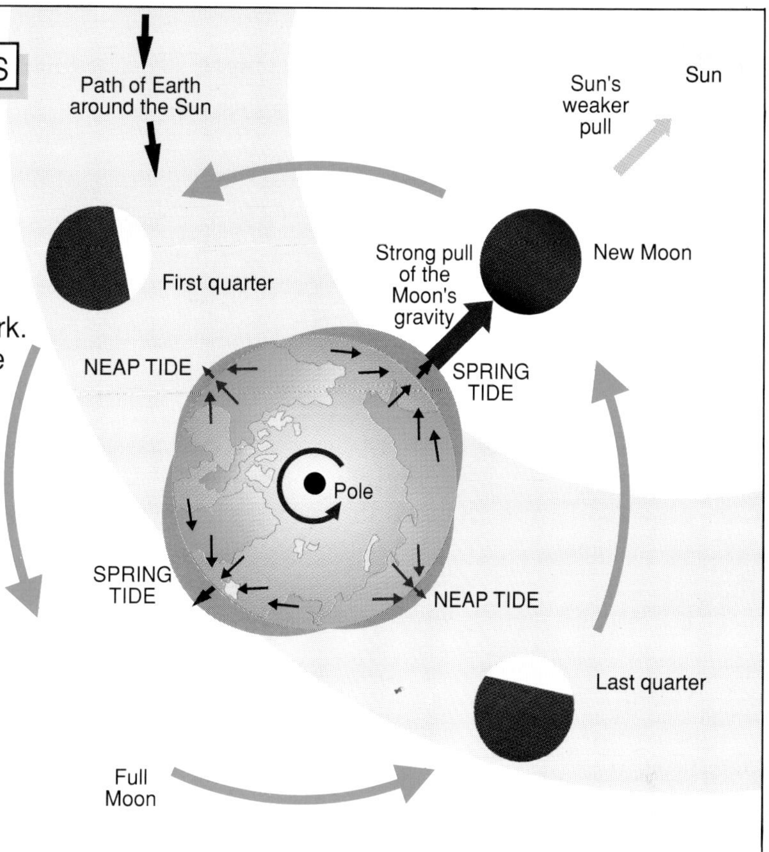

Path of Earth around the Sun

Sun's weaker pull

Sun

First quarter

New Moon

Strong pull of the Moon's gravity

NEAP TIDE

SPRING TIDE

Pole

SPRING TIDE

NEAP TIDE

Last quarter

Full Moon

**A** Semi-diurnal tides over 24 hours

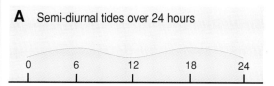

0   6   12   18   24

The Sun's gravity also pulls at the oceans but not as strongly as the Moon because the Sun is much further away. When the Moon and Sun are in line they act together so the bulges are higher. These are called **spring tides.** When the Moon and the Sun are at right angles, their pull works against one another, so the tides are lower. These are called **neap tides.**

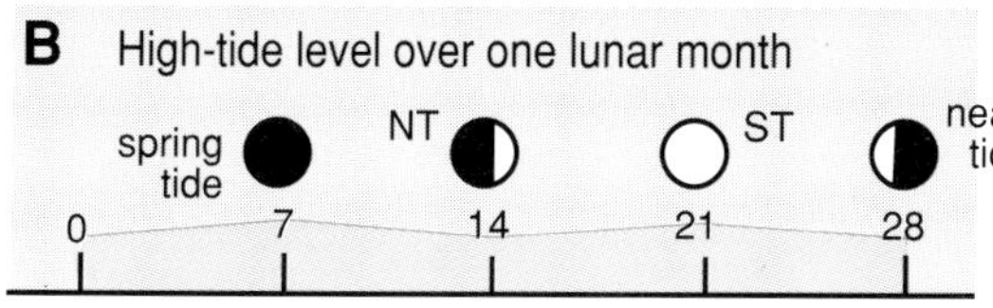

**B** High-tide level over one lunar month

spring tide   NT   ST   neap tide

0   7   14   21   28

From graph B you can see that there are two of each kind of tide in 28 days (1 lunar month).

1  What might be the disadvantages of constructing a tidal power station? (If there were no serious problems there would be large numbers of them.)
2  Tidal power stations are very efficient. More than 90 per cent of the energy turning the turbines is changed into electricity. In coal and oil-fired power stations efficiency rarely exceeds 70 per cent. Suggest some reasons for this difference.

### Key words

**coastal wetlands** – coastal environments where the ground is constantly waterlogged and frequently flooded by sea water.
**docks** – enclosures with gates to keep the water inside at a constant level.
**estuary** – the mouth of a river where the tide enters.
**gravitational potential energy** – this is the stored energy which anything has if it is at a higher level than something else. It is converted to the energy of movement (kinetic energy) when it falls down. For example, water stored behind a dam or a tidal barrage can be used to turn turbines when it is allowed to flow to a lower level.
For definitions of **potential** and **solar energy** see glossary.

# CHAPTER THREE

# AT THE EDGE OF THE OCEANS

The enormous power of the oceans is almost completely outside our control. Just as we cannot control earthquakes, tsunamis and hurricanes, so we cannot control currents, waves and tides.

It is at the edges of the oceans that we are most aware of this enormous power. Here the coast is always either being attacked and eroded or being built up by deposition. This coastal zone is vital for two reasons:

1 It is here that **defences against the oceans are built up.** We have to work with the power of the oceans and not against it. For example, we must protect delicately balanced environments, such as dune coasts, that act as defences. Dunes are shown below and on page 21.

2 This coastal zone is vital for a second reason. **It includes some of the most valuable environments on Earth.** They

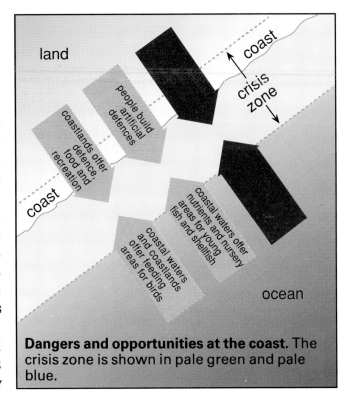

**Dangers and opportunities at the coast.** The crisis zone is shown in pale green and pale blue.

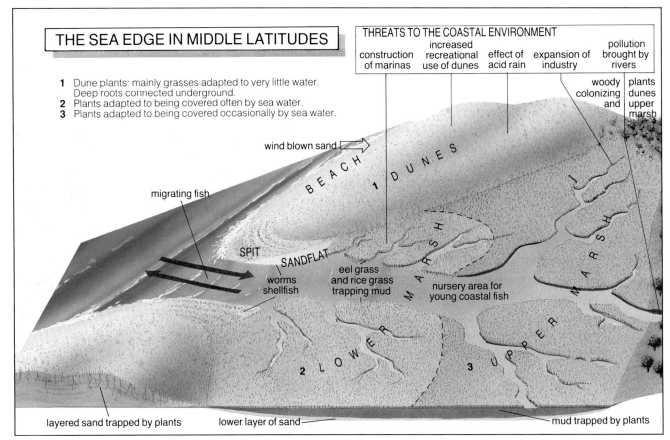

## THE SEA EDGE IN MIDDLE LATITUDES

1 Dune plants: mainly grasses adapted to very little water. Deep roots connected underground.
2 Plants adapted to being covered often by sea water.
3 Plants adapted to being covered occasionally by sea water.

THREATS TO THE COASTAL ENVIRONMENT

construction of marinas — increased recreational use of dunes — effect of acid rain — expansion of industry — pollution brought by rivers

woody colonizing and plants dunes upper marsh

wind blown sand

migrating fish

BEACH — DUNES

SPIT
SANDFLAT

worms shellfish

eel grass and rice grass trapping mud

nursery area for young coastal fish

MARSH

2 LOWER MARSH

3 UPPER MARSH

layered sand trapped by plants — lower layer of sand — mud trapped by plants include cliffs, beaches, dunes, marshes and mangrove swamps.

Some of the dangers and opportunities in these coastal zones are shown in the diagram on page 20.

## SAND-DUNE COASTS

Where the ocean builds up sandy beaches the wind can pick up the sand grains and spread them inland. But before the grains have travelled very far they meet land plants and other obstacles which stop them. The sand begins to pile up as dunes. Some plants have become specially adapted both to trap moving sand and to live on it as it builds up. It is these plants that fix the dunes in place.

Because sand is very porous, one of the main problems these plants have is how to get and keep water. Even though there may be plenty of rainfall these plants are faced with conditions in the soil which are quite like a desert.

Plants which grow in conditions of little water are named **xerophilous**, which means drought-loving. The most important of these in temperate lands are grasses. Their leaves are tough and may have a thick waterproof covering named a cuticle. Their leaves may also be rolled up into spikes to protect them from losing too much water. Their roots may be very long and deep, with lots of fine branches both to collect water and bind the loose sand grains. A good example is marram grass. It can grow new side shoots **above** the old ones as new sand accumulates. So as a dune builds up over the years the marram grasses grow with it and hold the layers of sand in place. (See the diagram on page 20.)

Unfortunately, dunes can be easily damaged by careless use. Examples are shown in the two photographs below. Both were taken on Holy Island, Northumberland, England. Other threats to dunes are from holiday-home building and from **acid rain**.

Plants and sand, and the dunes they build, provide coastal protection for very little cost. Their misuse by people seems a particularly foolish response to a valuable environment.

As the diagram on page 20 shows, dunes usually run parallel to the coast. When they are fixed, they form part of the natural coastal defences and also allow the development of other environments behind them. Some of these are discussed on page 22.

**Restoring a partly destroyed dune.** This dune was severely damaged by holidaymakers. It is being restored by using fencing to keep people out and to trap sand. New marram grass will be planted and the dune sides will steepen and become stable once more.

**Coastal dune with marram grass.** The dune has been damaged by visitors making footpaths through the grass. Bare sand is exposed. If the wind picks up this sand the whole dune will begin to blow away. This is named a 'blow-out'.

# THE WETLANDS

The diagram on page 20 shows how the shallow water behind dunes and sandspits provides another set of environments. The sheltered conditions provide environments for a wide variety of plants. They are all adapted to live in salt water or brackish water (mixed salt and fresh water). Plants such as cord grass and rice grass, (*Spartina* species) or the little glasswort (*Salicornia*) trap the mud and sand. As the trapped sediment builds up into mounds the water drains away and the mounds become the homes for other plant types that can colonize them. As these wetlands evolve the mounds of trapped sediment grow sideways as well as upwards. They begin to join together but leave channels between some of them for water to flow in and out with the tide.

Some parts of the marsh grow so high that only the highest tides cover them. As a result there is an upper and lower salt marsh as shown in the diagram on page 20. The left-hand photograph on this page shows a large area of salt marsh behind a dune coast.

In tropical lands, on sheltered shores where there is a lot of sand and mud, very different plants are found. They are mangrove trees and bushes. **Mangrove** is a name for a number of different plants adapted to living in waterlogged ground. They have roots which carry projections above the sand so they can get oxygen at low tide. (See the right-hand photograph below.)

On other tropical coasts, where waves are strong and the sand is frequently moved, coconut palms help to stabilize the shifting sands. In the Pacific and Indian Oceans, coconut palms help keep coral islands and atolls stable. **Atolls**, which are rings of coral formed around old volcanoes, may be only a few metres above sea level. Without the palms and other plants many of these atolls and islands would soon be destroyed by the sea. (See the photograph on page 23.)

All these temperate and tropical wetlands are very important to the life of the inshore marine environments. They are nurseries for young fish and shellfish which later mature at sea. They also trap many of the minerals which are washed from the land along with the mud. This makes the environment even richer.

The wetlands, like the sand-dunes, are easily damaged. But unlike the dunes they

**Salt marsh at Holy Island, Northumberland.** These students are working in a large area of salt marsh behind a line of coastal dunes. The tidal channel here is very shallow as it is at the extreme end of the tidal reach. In other marshes nearer the sea, channels may be metres deep.

**Mangroves, Red Sea, Saudi Arabia.** The sharp points of the aerial roots can be seen.

**Coral Islands, The Maldives, Indian Ocean.** The form of these low-lying atolls and reefs is very clear. Many islands like these are threatened by rising sea levels.

can be turned into rich farmland. They have to be drained and treated by growing plants which extract the salt from the soil. Much of the Netherlands has been reclaimed from the sea in this way. The Dutch name these reclaimed areas **polders.**

In the industrial world many marshlands have been reclaimed not for agriculture but for industry or leisure developments. In several parts of Europe and North America the wetlands are also being used for marinas and housing.

This destruction of the wetlands is interfering with the many inter-related environments of the coasts. Young fish can no longer breed nor can migrating birds feed there. Many shellfish have been wiped out along much of these coasts. This is not only the direct result of building on the wetlands. It is also the indirect result of pollution by industrial wastes pumped into the coastal waters. (See photograph on page 39.) The delicate but vital balance of nature is destroyed. At the same time the land is becom-ing more open to attack by the waves and tides, and has to be protected by very expensive artificial defences.

### Key words

**acid rain** – all rainwater should only be a *weak* acid. But it is turned into a *strong* acid when pollution in the atmosphere adds gases which dissolve in it.
**atoll** – a ring of coral reef growing round the stump of an old volcano or isolated rocky projection. They are found only in tropical and sub-tropical seas.
**mangroves** – tropical and sub-tropical trees adapted to being rooted in sea water.
**polder** – an enclosed area of land reclaimed from the sea.
**pollution** – the destruction of a healthy and balanced environment by adding substances to it.

# ARTIFICIAL DEFENCES

How can we defend ourselves against the power of the oceans? Some of this power is shown in the photograph below.

This strong cliffed coast has been worn back by the combined attack of ocean and weather. Left behind is a group of stacks named the Apostles. Between the stacks and in front of the cliffs a broad, gently sloping platform has been carved by the ocean. This is named the wave-cut platform. It has a thin coating of sand and gravel.

The photograph below shows this process of cutting is continuing because few rock fragments survive at the base of the cliffs and stacks. The waves keep attacking this coast and breaking up the rocks. The small pieces are eventually broken down to sand and gravel. As time passes the stacks themselves will be cut down by the sea. The wave-cut platform will be smoothed over by erosion. **The power of the oceans is not only very great it is persistent as well.**

Artificial defences of many kinds have been built to try and restrain this power. Most of them succeed for only a short time. On page 25 are two photographs of sea walls. One sea wall, in France, appears to be a successful defence. The second has been completely destroyed. The second wall is in Guadeloupe where hurricane conditions are quite common (see page 14). In November 1984, Hurricane Klaus destroyed many sea defences including this one. Not only was the wave attack very violent but it also succeeded in getting behind the artificial defence and attacking the softer rocks. The wall was battered from the front and undermined from the back at the same time.

**Cliff coast with stacks, Brittany, France.**

**The effects of a wave attack on sea walls.**
Effective sea defence on the French coast (left) and total destruction in Guadaloupe (right).

Some lowland coasts are threatened not only by wave attack but also by storm surges. A storm surge occurs when violent winds 'pile up' water on one side of a sea or ocean. If a storm surge occurs at the same time as an exceptionally high tide large areas of lowland may be drowned. This has happened several times in the Thames estuary in England. To prevent this happening again the Thames Flood Barrier was constructed in the 1980s. When a weather forecast warns of an easterly storm surge moving towards southeast England the barriers can be raised. This will prevent the estuary and Central London being flooded.

Two factors will make even this huge defence work a failure in the future. Firstly, southeast England, along with North Belgium and much of the Netherlands is slowly sinking into the North Sea. Secondly, if the Greenhouse Effect (see pages 39 and 40) develops much further world sea levels may rise by several metres in the next 50 years. The Thames flood barrier will become completely useless.

**The Thames Flood Barrier, near Greenwich.** The sections of the barrier rest on the river bed to allow shipping to pass. The barriers can be lifted up by the yellow cranes on the islands. One section is being raised. The control centre is in the foreground.

# CHAPTER FOUR

# RESOURCES OF THE OCEANS

## FISHING

In the last 25 years it has become obvious that we need to work **with** the oceans when we take fish from them.

Our greed for fish has almost wiped out several species. The same is true of the way we have destroyed most of the whales. Only now, when it is almost too late, are we learning two important lessons about working with the oceans.

1 The fishing resources of the sea must be **farmed** rather than **mined**. This means that instead of treating fish like coal, taking out until supplies are exhausted, we have to farm the fish. For example:
   a) catches must be restricted, especially of young fish,
   b) we must actively encourage fish breeding, and protect the breeding grounds.
2 Working with the oceans can only be effective if it is carried out by **international agreements and controls.** For example, there is no point in most of the whaling countries giving up whaling if one or two continue to catch whales in large numbers. This is even more important **now** than in the past. So few whales have survived our greed they could now be wiped out by the actions of just a few countries.

The need for international co-operation is also important because many valuable species of fish, such as tuna, migrate over great distances. One of these major patterns, for the big-eye tuna in the Pacific Ocean, is shown in the map on page 27. This fish is caught by all the Pacific fishing nations. International co-operation is the only way to control catches.

The map on page 27 shows the position of the world's major tuna fisheries. In these areas there is plenty of food for the zooplankton and for the fish that feed on them.

In contrast there are the areas shaded yellow which are **marine deserts**. Here there are few plankton so these areas are poor habitats for fish. These areas are the coldest and the warmest oceans.

**A pair of Baleen Whales off the coast of Alaska.**

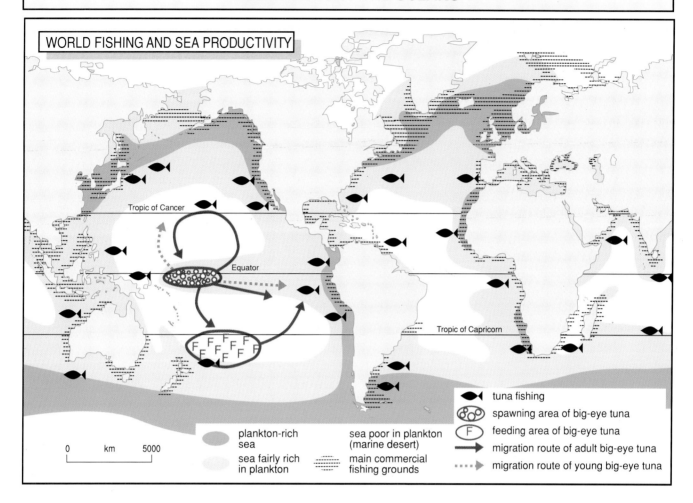

WORLD FISHING AND SEA PRODUCTIVITY

Tropic of Cancer

Equator

Tropic of Capricorn

0 km 5000

tuna fishing
spawning area of big-eye tuna
feeding area of big-eye tuna
migration route of adult big-eye tuna
migration route of young big-eye tuna

plankton-rich sea
sea fairly rich in plankton
sea poor in plankton (marine desert)
main commercial fishing grounds

Deep water fishing fleets are highly specialized. They can stay at sea for weeks at a time. Many boats carry sound echo equipment (sonar) to locate their catches. This sends out pulses of sound which are reflected back from the sea-bed. When a shoal of fish is in line with the signal the echo is returned in a much shorter time. This tells the captain when to lower his nets.

There are three main kinds of deep ocean ships operating around the world. They are the giant **purse seiner**, the oceanic **long-liner** and the **factory trawler.** The first is used by American and Japanese fleets to catch tuna fish. As you can see from the map, tuna fish are very widespread. Purse seiners fish all the oceans. The purse seine net is a huge wide-mouthed net towed behind the ship. It can catch a whole school of tuna at one time. Many of these ships are based in California, Japan and Korea. Unfortunately, they also scoop up large numbers of dolphins which feed on tuna. Over 150 000 of these beautiful animals are killed in this way each

year in the Eastern Pacific. This slaughter, together with the many killed by pollution around the world threatens the whole future of these animals.

The long-liner comes mainly from eastern Asia, especially Japan and South Korea. This ship catches fish on baited lines which may be over 20km (12½ miles) long. One ship may pull three lines. As the baited hooks are only a metre apart this kind of fishing requires a lot of labour. As dolphins are slaughtered for bait this kind of fishing is yet one more threat to their futures.

The factory trawler has been developed especially by the USSR and other eastern European countries. (See the photograph on page 29.) Each ship is a self-contained catcher and factory in which all the fish are gutted and frozen. Fleets of these ships cover many thousands of kilometres fishing in Antarctic waters, around the Falkland Islands, the Pacific and South African coasts. They can take and process almost every kind of fish they find.

The fishing industry of the world relies on very few kinds of animals for its resources. Less than 40 types of marine animals account for nearly 75 per cent of the world's catch. The most important of these types are cod, mackerel, herring, sardine and anchovy, plus the non-fish types of squid and krill (a tiny shrimp-like animal). Cod, mackerel, herring and squid are for human consumption. The others are regarded as industrial fish which are processed **both** for human uses and for animal feed.

It used to be thought that krill could be taken in unlimited quantities but US scientists showed that the krill is not as abundant as everyone thought. This means that krill could be overfished. Whales and other animals which depend on them as food in Antarctica could face starvation. (See **Last Frontiers, Polar Lands.**)

The growth of the world's fishing fleets, concentrated on so few fish types, carries with it all the dangers of **overfishing**. When this happens the amount of fish caught gets less and the fish are younger and smaller. This has become marked in many fishing grounds, for example, the North Sea and coastal Peru.

Overfishing can develop very quickly because fish reproduction can be a risky business. For example, in the Bering Sea, fish lay eggs at times which match two rapid growths or **blooms** of plankton each year. The eggs drift towards these bloom areas carried by the current so that when the young fish hatch they will have plenty of food. However, the failure rate is high and in a poor year there may be a much lower production of young fish. **But the fishing remains the same so the population of the fish is cut back.** It may take several good years for the fish population to recover.

Another example is provided by the Atlantic salmon. This fish breeds in the rivers of northwest Europe, especially Scotland, Norway and Ireland. They migrate to sea to feed in the northwest Atlantic Ocean near Greenland. For many years the migration route was not known. But when research discovered it, unscrupulous fishermen moved in and fewer and fewer fish managed to migrate back to their home rivers. To make matters worse the salmon were affected by disease in the 1960s. As a result the stocks have declined and in many rivers the salmon is near to **extinction**.

**Fish killed by pollution.** In the rivers and seas of industrialized countries fish stocks are being reduced by pollution as well as by overfishing (see above).

**A modern fishing vessel off the coast of Scotland.** FV Wave Crest pumping fish on board. Modern fishing boats can take larger catches than older boats. They can also handle the catches much faster.

**Fishing vessels at the Scottish Coast.** A variety of different vessels can be seen. In the centre is a large Russian ship, referred to by the fishermen as a klondyker. It takes on board the catches of the smaller vessels. The fish can be stored in deep freezes or processed before storage.

The serious effects of overfishing can run right through a whole food chain. In the early 1970s fishing for lobster on the coasts of Nova Scotia and eastern Canada, cut back the lobster population. But lobsters catch and eat sea urchins which in turn eat kelp seaweed. Because so many lobsters were caught the sea urchin population grew very large and ate up all the kelp. This left them without any food. So the lobsters, the urchins, the kelp and the fishermen all suffered from overfishing.

It is crises like these which have led to better understanding of what is happening to our oceans. This has led to developing the opportunity for much closer co-operation between the fishing countries of the world. Some countries have extended the boundary of the ocean water they claim. Inside this boundary they now keep a close watch on fish stocks. They control their own fishing and that of other countries to which they sell fishing licences.

In other examples, countries grouped round a particular ocean or sea manage the fish stocks as a shared operation. The North Sea provides a good example of this kind of management (but see page 36). At present the EEC countries plus Norway, Sweden, Poland and the USSR have about 45 000 fishing boats catching fish in this sea. But the operations are controlled by a strict quota system. This system is not only concerned with the total number of fish caught but also with the numbers and ages of each of the main types of fish. For example, net sizes and designs are carefully controlled so that very young fish can escape.

**Key words**

**blooms** – rapid growths of phytoplankton.
**extinction** – the complete destruction of a species with no survivors.
**overfishing** – taking fish from the sea or river to the point where the stock is not replacing itself. If overfishing is not checked it will lead to the extinction of that species of fish.

# MINERALS FROM THE SEA-BED

The world demand for minerals for industry continues to grow. One result is that people are exploring the possibilities of mining minerals from under the sea-bed. So far most of the developments have been restricted to shallow waters. Mining is concentrated on the continental shelves and in the shallow seas like the North Sea. We do not have the technology to extract minerals from under very deep waters. Even if we had it the expense would be too great to make mining worthwhile.

The major developments in recent years have been in extracting oil and gas from the rocks of the sea floor. Both the drilling and pumping are done from platforms. These platforms either rest on the sea floor on long legs, or they float while tethered by cables. The photograph below shows the scene at a gas platform.

In the North Sea huge quantities of gas and oil are now being mined. The reserves there have proved much larger than was originally believed.

The map on page 31 shows the positions of some of the world's mineral resources in the sea-beds. Many of these minerals are also available on land. But as they are used up so the possibility of mining the sea floors becomes more attractive.

Some of the solid minerals obtained from the sea floor are dredged up in shallow water. These deposits have been concentrated in particular places by the action of ocean currents and rivers. They are named placer deposits; examples include tin and gold. The diagram on page 31 shows how they have been formed and how they are dredged up. The other valuable materials obtained in much the same way are the large quantities of sand and gravel dredged up for the building industry.

**The Kinsale gas platform** photographed from the service ship in the foreground. In the distance a gas carrier is being loaded. Why are helicopters important in the North Sea oil and gas fields?

# RESOURCES OF THE OCEANS

## SOME OCEANIC MINERAL SOURCES AND MAJOR SUPERTANKER ROUTES

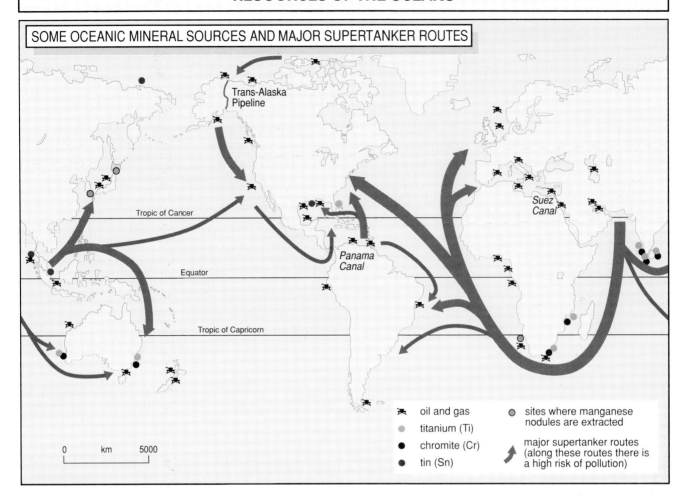

Trans-Alaska Pipeline

Tropic of Cancer

Equator

Tropic of Capricorn

Panama Canal

Suez Canal

0    km    5000

| | oil and gas | | sites where manganese nodules are extracted |
| | titanium (Ti) | | |
| | chromite (Cr) | | major supertanker routes (along these routes there is a high risk of pollution) |
| | tin (Sn) | | |

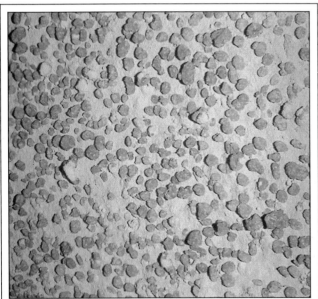

**Manganese nodules on the sea-bed.** These nodules contain manganese and also as much as 20 per cent iron and 6 per cent aluminium. Other valuable minerals are also included in much smaller quantities. Unfortunately, most of the large collections of these nodules are in waters too deep to be dredged. New technology will have to be invented before that is possible.

## FORMATION OF PLACER DEPOSITS

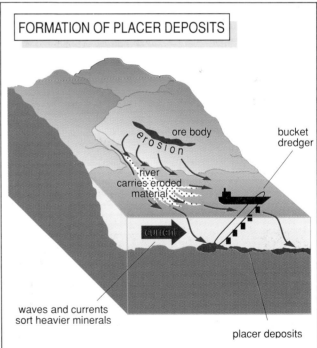

ore body

bucket dredger

erosion

river carries eroded material

current

waves and currents sort heavier minerals

placer deposits

Metal deposits on land are eroded by rivers. The grains are then carried out to sea. The action of river and sea currents concentrates the heavier minerals as placer deposits. If these are in shallow water they can be mined by bucket dredgers.

# TREASURE FROM THE DEEP

The technology for underwater exploration is changing rapidly. (See the photograph on page 5.) As we develop better ways of moving and working under water, large areas of the sea floor can be reached for treasure hunting and marine archaeology. However, it is important to remember that we can only reach the floor of the shallower seas and the continental shelf (see diagram on page 6). It is sea-floor work rather than ocean-floor work.

Some discoveries are very exciting and make headline news, for example, discovery of sunken treasure. An example is shown in the two photographs on page 33. One picture is of part of the treasure itself, the other is of a model of the treasure ship. The "Atocha" treasure wreck was brought to the surface near Key West, Florida, USA in the mid-1980s.

Sometimes underwater discoveries may not seem as exciting as treasure. For example, the photograph below shows a find of pottery. But these man-made objects (artifacts) are also very valuable. They tell us about the ways in which people lived in the past. Sometimes a particular find will completely change our ideas about our ancestors. One example, was the find, in the Aegean Sea, of an ancient Greek mechanical computer which gave the position of important navigational markers such as stars. This find showed the ancient world was much more advanced than we had thought.

Ancient timbers rot easily when they are taken out of the sea. To preserve them scientists have had to develop many chemicals and processes to help them survive. For example, in the 1980s the remains of Henry VIII's great warship, the "Mary Rose" was raised from the depths of Southampton Water in southern England. The preservation of its fragile remains has taken years of work. These new methods of preservation can now be applied to many other situations where rot might occur. This is a good example of how working with the sea can provide valuable new knowledge.

As scientists develop new ways of working safely in deeper waters many more treasures will come within our reach.

**Marine archaeology.** The wreck of an ancient Greek cargo ship with its cargo of jars (amphorae). We can learn a lot about how people lived in the past by studying these everyday objects.

**A treasure ship.** One of the ways marine archaeologists share their finds with other people is by setting up a museum. Here some American children are looking at a model of the "Atocha" treasure ship.

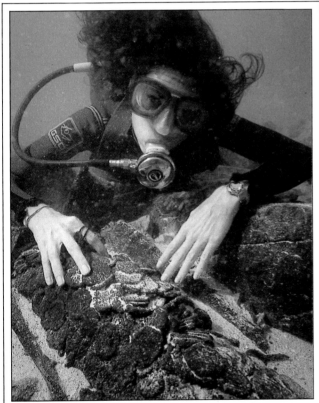

**A diver with gold bars and coins at the discovery of the treasure ship "Atocha" off the Florida Coast.** The simple equipment worn by the diver shows that the wreck is in shallow water. (Compare this photograph with the one on page 5.)

**Key words**

**artifact** – any man-made object.
**marine archaeology** – scientific investigation of man-made objects in the sea.

1 The 'popular phrase' used at the top of page 32 is **Treasure from the Deep.** Explain why a more sensible phrase to use might be **Treasure from the Shallows.** Why do newspaper editors not use this heading?
2 Describe the difficulties that face marine archaeologists as they try to reach a sunken treasure ship. What are the several reasons why the work gets more difficult in deeper water?
3 Look through any reference books at home or at school or in a library to find out more about recovering sunken ships. You may like to concentrate on one particular wreck and make up a scrapbook about it.

# SHIPS

The discovery and use of ocean resources has depended on the development of ships. It is also a helpful idea to think of the oceans themselves as 'transport resources'. Much of the history of the world has been decided by the uses made of the oceans as routeways.

The diagram on page 35 shows some of the types of ships constructed in the past. Also shown are some modern ship designs. Whatever the age of these ships, their designers and users have been concerned with the two main problems of safety and efficiency.

## 1 Safety

As ships have become larger and more solidly built, usually of metal instead of wood, they have become safer. Very large ships can now survive all but the very worst ocean storms. Modern navigation aids and more accurate weather forecasting also help make sea travel much safer.

## 2 Efficiency

Efficiency has improved at the same time as safety has increased. The most efficient ships use the least fuel for their size, have fewer crew members and may also travel quicker.

Efficiency is being improved in many ways but three methods are especially important.

**a) Ships are designed to be more specialized.**

General cargo-carrying boats are now quite rare and usually small. The main shipping routes are now travelled by

**Container ship and the container dock, Seattle, USA.** This ship is typical of the highly specialized ship designs of today. Also specially designed are the ways of handling the cargo, and in moving the containers by road to and from container docks.

supertankers, bulk carriers, container ships, ferries, cruise liners and oil platform service ships. (See photographs on pages 29, 30 and 34.)

## b) Modern use of old designs.

A major cost for shipping is caused by drag. This is friction between the ship and the water. A modern supertanker uses half its fuel in overcoming drag. Drag is made much worse if the ship is moved sideways in the water by the waves or if it rolls too easily. Designs which reduce these effects also reduce costs.

The catamaran ship with twin hulls is very stable and moves efficiently through the water. The cruise liner "Phoenix World City" has twin hulls like the Polynesian cargo boat. The twin hulls plus aerofoil stabilizers mean that this very tall ship is not blown over sideways nor pushed off course. Passengers can be embarked from ferry boats in the calm water between the two hulls. This modern ship is hundreds of times larger than the Polynesian boat but the basic design is the same.

## c) New designs.

A modern ship looks very unlike the Greek ship in the picture. But ships of the future may also look very unlike our ships.

One area of new design is in making better use of wind power. For example, experiments are being carried out with the Walker Wing Sail (see picture). This sail is based on the design of aircraft wings and makes efficient use of wind energy.

The Japanese ship, "Shinaitoku Maru" carries sails made of lightweight metal. Their position is always being varied by computers using information about wind strength and direction. Fuel costs have been cut by 20 per cent. In a beam sea (from the side) when waves and wind tip other ships to one side, the "Shinaitoku Maru" remains steady. No power is wasted by constantly trying to straighten the ship.

EXAMPLES OF ANCIENT AND MODERN SHIP DESIGN

Dug-out boat

A reed boat from ancient Egypt

A Polynesian catamaran

A Greek ship

the cruise liner Phoenix World City

aerofoil stabilizers

Walker Wing Sail

the motor vessel Shinaitoku Maru

BEAM SEA

(Not drawn to scale.)

# CHAPTER FIVE

# THE OCEANS IN CRISIS

## POLLUTION

The oceans and seas of the world are in crisis. **A major cause of this crisis is pollution.** The peoples of the world are polluting the waters of the world with their sewage, agricultural chemicals and the waste products of industry. (See the photographs on pages 28 and 39.)

**The greatest damage is being caused by the richest countries.** These are the industrial countries such as Japan, USA, West Germany and the UK. They are now being joined in this process of destruction by countries developing their industries to the same level. These countries include the USSR, Canada, Australia and Brazil.

Pollution effects are most marked in the seas surrounded by industrialized countries. These include the North Sea, the Irish Sea, the Mediterranean, the Inland Sea of Japan, the Black Sea, the Caspian Sea and the Sea of Azov. In the Sea of Azov the total annual catch of fish was once over 300 000 tonnes. Now it is reduced to a low-quality catch of 3000 tonnes.

The dangers are now very clear but so are the opportunities. They are to reduce pollution and to research ways of undoing some of the damage already done. In both the Mediterranean and the North Sea, international agreements now exist to control and reduce the release of wastes. Unfortunately, there are two reasons why progress is sometimes dangerously slow:

1 Despite the evidence, some countries are still reluctant to accept the need for immediate action. For example, the UK still dumps huge quantities of sewage sludge into the North Sea and Irish Sea, as well as releasing untreated sewage. It is the view of the UK Government that the seriousness of the pollution of the North Sea has not yet been proved. Apparently, the proof required by the UK will only be available when the North Sea is totally destroyed. In the Netherlands, an attempt by the government to pass strong anti-pollution laws in May 1989 led to the Government having to resign. Other parties would not support the increase in taxes to pay for the clean-up.

2 The sheer volume of the **pollutants** means that very rapid improvements are not possible. For example, the River Rhine puts the following tonnes of toxic wastes into the North Sea **every year**:

| | | |
|---|---|---|
| Cadmium | 10 | Plus smaller quantities |
| Chromium | 360 | of even more dangerous wastes such as mercury |
| Copper | 235 | and arsenic. Some |
| Lead | 185 | agricultural chemicals carried to the sea are |
| Zinc | 1500 | known to cause cancer. |

It will take many years to reduce pollution to safe, low levels, and even longer to stop it completely.

Pollution is most concentrated in the seas and the ocean edges close to industrial countries. But because the oceans are connected to each other many pollutants spread round the world. They spread in three main ways:

1 Pollutants are carried in the atmosphere and then dropped into the oceans. An example of a natural pollutant is ash from volcanic eruptions. An example of chemical pollution is smoke from power stations which returns to land and sea as acid rain.

2 Pollutants are carried in ocean currents. For example, shallow coastal waters where shellfish breed are polluted by city wastes. These wastes are carried into the sea by rivers. Coastal currents then transfer the wastes along the coast to the shellfish areas.

## SOME CAUSES OF POLLUTION IN THE OCEANS

METAL INDUSTRIES

CHEMICAL INDUSTRIES

TOWNS

FARMING

nitrates phosphates

sewage

heavy metals

chemicals

R I V E R   B A S I N

nuclear power and waste processing

mining and quarrying

sea birds

oil spillage

burning industrial waste

industrial waste

sewage solid and liquid wastes

oil slick

oil spillage

radioactive elements

ALGAL BLOOMS

SHELLFISH

ZOOPLANKTON

MAMMALS

PHYTOPLANKTON

FISH

DUMPED SEWAGE SLUDGE

Much of the pollution which passes from land to sea is carried by rivers. Rivers carry effluents, or waste water, from homes and factories. Rain washes some pollutants off fields and into the rivers, and some flows directly into the sea from coastal towns, factories, mines, ships and nuclear power stations. Once in the sea, pollutants enter the food chain and some can be blown back onto the land in fine sea spray and the remains of algal blooms.

Poorer countries may not produce the same kinds of pollutants. However, many poorer countries are cutting down jungles and forests. This leads to soil erosion. As a result, huge quantities of sand and mud are being dumped into the sea by the rivers.

3 Pollutants enter the food chains in the oceans. Pollutants are taken in by the phytoplankton, passed on to the zooplankton, then on to fish and other sea creatures. Eventually, some of these pollutants find their way back into people's diets. We are all being poisoned by our own wastes.

Some of the causes of pollution and the links between them are shown on page 37.

**The spread of pollutants throughout the oceans makes the crisis an international crisis.** A dramatic example of this was discovered in the 1950s. The insecticide DDT was used in many *tropical countries* to kill mosquitoes and so check the spread of malaria. But within a very short time DDT was detected in the fish, the seals and the birds of the *polar seas.*

There have been many other examples like this. They show us that the only effective controls are international controls. It is vital that the wealthy industrial countries use some of their wealth to reduce their own pollution. But they must also help their poorer neighbours to avoid the same mistakes as they develop their agriculture and industry.

**The enemies of progress are greed and ignorance.**

Greedy companies may choose to go on polluting the rivers and oceans so they can keep their profits. They will only stop when government scientists prove they are doing this, and when very large fines are imposed by the courts.

The second enemy is ignorance. We do not really understand the full seriousness of the damage we are causing. Effective control of pollution depends on accurate information.

Ignorance is the enemy in other ways. It encourages the greedy and stupid to go on polluting the world. They say things like: 'If it was **really** causing harm we would know'. But would we? Do we really know the damaging effects of pollution in the ocean depths? How unsafe are the oceans becoming?

The other attitude encouraged by ignorance is that of 'out of sight: out of mind'. One of the worst examples of this is the use of incinerator ships. These ships sail onto the ocean packed with refuse. This refuse is burned at sea and the ash dumped into the water. This probably causes as much pollution as if it had happened on land. But because it cannot be seen it has been ignored. This dangerous practice is now being outlawed but it will be some years before it is stopped completely.

**Deep ocean fish.** This rare fish lives at depth in the oceans. The light organs below the eye give out both ordinary and red light. This fish can see red animals otherwise invisible in the depths.

## POLLUTION AND THE GREENHOUSE EFFECT

The atmosphere and oceans of the world are very closely linked (see chapter 2). These links are now entering a new stage because of the effects of pollution.

The peoples of the world are adding gases to the atmosphere at a far faster rate than ever before. These gases include:

a) carbon dioxide from the burning of coal, oil, gas and wood. This includes car fuels and the burning of the world's jungles.

b) CFC gases (chlorofluorocarbons) which are used in aerosols, refrigerators and some plastics.

c) methane and other gases from decaying materials, and from human and animal wastes.

d) nitrous oxides from fertilizers and vehicle exhausts.

These gases are collecting in the upper atmosphere faster then they can be naturally dispersed. It is this build-up of gases that is creating the **greenhouse effect**. This is explained in the diagram on the right.

This interference with the atmosphere is also damaging the oceans in two ways:

1 Phytoplankton play a major role in the production of carbon dioxide. This role will be changed by the increased amounts of carbon dioxide available. Any significant change in the phytoplankton will affect all parts of ocean food chains (see page 9).

2 Oceans are warmed by the greenhouse effect. There is evidence that the Polar ice sheets may be melting faster. In both the north and south Atlantic larger icebergs are now breaking off from the main ice. In several places in northern Canada the glacier ice is melting faster. If this continues then sea level will rise.

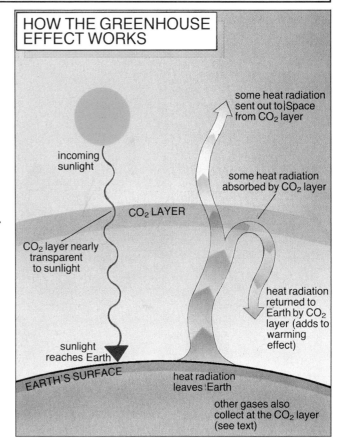

HOW THE GREENHOUSE EFFECT WORKS

incoming sunlight

$CO_2$ layer nearly transparent to sunlight

$CO_2$ LAYER

sunlight reaches Earth

EARTH'S SURFACE

some heat radiation sent out to Space from $CO_2$ layer

some heat radiation absorbed by $CO_2$ layer

heat radiation returned to Earth by $CO_2$ layer (adds to warming effect)

heat radiation leaves Earth

other gases also collect at the $CO_2$ layer (see text)

**Pipe blocking action by Greenpeace at Portman.** This pipe was blocked as a protest. It dumps industrial waste into the Mediterranean. The wastes include cadmium, lead, zinc, cyanide and sulphuric acid.

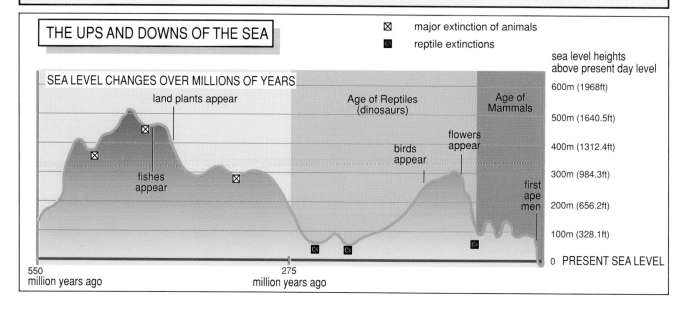

THE UPS AND DOWNS OF THE SEA

⊠ major extinction of animals
▨ reptile extinctions

sea level heights
above present day level

SEA LEVEL CHANGES OVER MILLIONS OF YEARS

land plants appear

Age of Reptiles
(dinosaurs)

Age of Mammals

600m (1968ft)

500m (1640.5ft)

flowers appear

400m (1312.4ft)

birds appear

300m (984.3ft)

fishes appear

first ape men

200m (656.2ft)

100m (328.1ft)

0 PRESENT SEA LEVEL

550 million years ago

275 million years ago

As the graph above shows there have been many changes of sea level in the history of the Earth. The most recent were those of the Ice Ages. But the present situation is unique. **It is the first time that pollution by the peoples of the world has played a major part in affecting sea level.** We do not know just how much harm we are doing.

The worst forecast from computer models is that in the next 50 years average Earth temperatures will rise by 4 – 5°C (10°F). This will cause a rise of sea level of between 5m (16 ft) and 10m (32 ft). Lower figures are a temperature rise of 3°C (7°F) leading to a sea level rise of 1.68m (5.5 ft) by the year 2030.

Even at the **lower** forecasts the results will be serious. In Egypt 8 million people could be made homeless and a quarter of all croplands might be drowned. In Bangladesh 20 millions could lose their homes and farms. In the UK 15 million homes might be lost, while it is doubtful if much of the Netherlands could survive. Much of the east coast of the USA would be flooded. At an **average** forecast all these areas would suffer still more damage. In addition 60 of the world's largest cities would be drowned.

It is no good waiting to see which forecast turns out to be correct. Worldwide pollution controls need to be in operation now, and they are not. There is not much time left.

**New York in AD 2030?**

### Key words

**pollutant** – any material, natural or man-made, which is added to an environment and damages it.
For definition of **pollution** see glossary.
**toxic wastes** – groups of pollutants which are known to be poisonous, e.g. lead and mercury.

# CONCLUSIONS

Working with the oceans requires **three aims:**

1 We have to find out more about the oceans and our place in their environments.

2 We have to stop abusing the riches of the oceans, and build a partnership with them.

3 If we believe these first two aims are right then our third aim is to fight for them. If we mean to protect the oceans we have to fight the greedy and selfish who are interested only in making profits. They do not care about the polluted inheritance they are leaving for their children and for yours.

To achieve these aims we must recognize **three facts:**

1 **The oceans are in a state of balance.** Despite the great power of the oceans this state of balance is often quite delicate. For example, in the North Sea (see page 6) the erosion of the cliffs of east Yorkshire and Lincolnshire provides much of the mud carried south by sea currents to build up the salt marshes of Belgium, the Netherlands, West Germany and Denmark. Controlling cliff erosion in eastern England has become an **international** matter of not upsetting this delicate state of balance.

A second example is found in the Great Barrier Reef of eastern Australia. Here the Crown of Thorns Starfish lives by eating coral. A few years ago the number of these starfish rapidly increased. The balance was upset and the coral began to be eaten away faster than it grew. Parts of the reef were in danger of disappearing. One of the causes of this was that shell collectors were catching too many of the sea creatures that kill and eat the starfish. If shell collecting is now controlled the balance may not be so much upset in the future.

**The Crown of Thorns Starfish.** This animal lives by eating coral. If its numbers increase it will destroy coral faster than it is replaced. Reefs and atolls may be eaten away.

**Sea-floor habitat with divers.** Experiments with ways of living underwater are very exciting. In the future we may see the creation of underwater cities. None of this is likely to happen if the oceans become severely polluted.

**2   The oceans are places of great potential.**

We have already seen how fishing and ocean travel can be improved and developed (see pages 26 to 29 and pages 34 and 35). The potential of proper fish farming is to give food for all for ever. The potential of modern sea travel is that all countries are better connected by safe routes and safe ships.

The other great potential is that the oceans are a source of power. Some of the methods of developing safe, clean power from the oceans were discussed on pages 17 and 18. But now an even bigger breakthrough seems possible in developing power from the oceans.

For several years scientists have been studying the possibility of using deuterium, a form of hydrogen, to produce cheap electricity. Deuterium is found in sea-water. The problem has been that the process, nuclear fusion, is highly dangerous and very expensive. But recently, two scientists, Fleischmann and Pons, have claimed they carried out this process in a relatively cheap and safe laboratory experiment. If this experiment can be developed then sea-water will provide us with unlimited cheap power. One bucket of sea-water contains enough deuterium to make the same amount of energy as 10 tonnes of coal. However, many other scientists are not convinced by the experiment.

**3   The oceans are now in crisis.**

This is the result of misuse by the peoples of the world. Unless we can agree quickly amongst ourselves to stop pollution, and to clear up the pollution already committed, most of the potential of the oceans will be lost for ever.

The danger is that the oceans are being ruined.

The opportunity is that we know this is so and have a last chance to co-operate internationally to stop this destruction. It is now a battle between the conservationists and the exploiters.

**Greenpeace protest.** This Greenpeace inflatable boat was destroyed by two barrels of nuclear waste dropped by the Dutch dumping ship, the "Rijnborg". This is a battle between conservationists and exploiters. This time no one was killed. But what will happen when barrels of nuclear waste start rusting and leaking?

# GLOSSARY

**abyssal plain** – the deep ocean floor beyond the continental slope.

**atoll** – a ring of coral reef in a tropical or subtropical sea.

**blooms** – rapid growth of phytoplankton.

**blow hole** – a hole eroded right through a cliff. Air blows out of the top of this as a wave enters the bottom.

**carbon dioxide** – a gas with one atom of carbon to two of oxygen. It is present in most life processes.

**chlorophyll** – the green pigment in plants which absorbs all light except green wavelengths. This is why plants which have it are green.

**conservation** – to save for the future the resources of an environment. To be most effective conservation needs rules, laws and agreements by governments.

**continental drift** – the slow movement of the continents as they are carried by the crustal plates.

**continental shelf** – the submerged edge of the continental plain.

**continental slope** – the gentle underwater slope at the edge of the continental shelf.

**crustal plate** – a rigid section of crustal rock.

**element** – a substance which cannot be split into any other substances.

**environment** – the surroundings of plants, animals and people. People can change an environment by caring for it or by misusing it.

**Equator** – nought degrees of latitude. The division between the northern and southern halves (the hemispheres) of the world.

**erosion** – the breakdown and removal of rocks and soils.

**estuary** – the tidal part of a river where it meets the sea.

**exploiters** – people who take from an environment for profit without putting anything back to conserve it, e.g. companies that overfish the seas, companies that dump nuclear waste in the oceans.

**extinction** – the complete destruction of a species with no survivors.

**eye** – calm centre of a hurricane.

**hurricane** – a violent rotating tropical storm.

**hydrogen** – the simplest element known.

**lava** – molten rock.

**magma** – intensely hot molten material in the interior of the earth.

**mangrove trees** – tropical and subtropical trees adapted to being rooted in salt water.

**ocean** – a great body of water occupying a major part of the Earth's surface.

**overfishing** – taking fish from the sea or river to the point where the stock is not replacing itself.

**oxygen** – the element needed for breathing, and which is used in the body to extract energy from food.

**photosynthesis** – the process in green plants of making food by using sunlight.

**phytoplankton** – very small plants, usually single-celled, which float and drift in the oceans.

**polder** – an enclosed area of land reclaimed from the sea.

**pollutant** – any material, natural or man-made which is added to an environment and damages it.

**pollution** – the destruction of a healthy and balanced environment by adding substances to it. These substances may be excessive amounts of what is already present naturally, e.g. mud. They may be chemicals which were originally not present at all, e.g. agricultural pesticides.

**potential energy** – this is stored energy which can be converted to the energy of movement (kinetic energy) to do work. For example, the stretched elastic in a catapult has stored energy which is released to propel a stone.

**predator** – a form of life that lives by hunting and eating another.

**sea** – a body of water close to or largely surrounded by land. (Sometimes confused with ocean and used interchangeably.)

**solar energy**– this is the energy of light radiated by the sun. It is used by plants to convert simple chemicals to food which has a lot of stored energy. When it is absorbed by solids, liquids or gases it is converted to heat energy.

**toxic wastes** – groups of pollutants which are known to be poisonous e.g. lead or mercury.

**tsunami** – earthquake or volcanic shock wave that passes through the ocean as a huge water wave.

**turbine** – an arrangement of turning blades mounted on a central shaft.

**water** – the liquid formed by the bonding of two molecules of hydrogen to one of oxygen: $H_2O$.

**zooplankton** – a group of tiny floating animals that live off the phytoplankton.

# FURTHER READING

## INTRODUCTORY BOOKS

Burton, R. *Atlas of the Sea* Heinemann 1974

Burton, R. et al. *The Living Sea* Orbis 1976

Campbell, A.C. *The Hamlyn Guide to the Seashore and Shallow Seas of Britain and Europe* Hamlyn 1976. This is a superbly illustrated, easily used guide to accessible marine life.

Cook, J. L. *The Mysterious Undersea World* National Geographic Society 1980

Lambert, D. *The Ocean* Ward Lock Ltd 1979

Thorson, G. *Life in the Sea* Weidenfeld and Nicholson 1971

## MORE ADVANCED READING

Barratt, J. M. and Yonge, C. M. *Collins Pocket Guide to the Seashore* Collins 1958. This is the book students and naturalists use for identifying common shore plants and animals.

Muns, R. J. and Dahlstrom, P. *Collins Guide to the Sea and Fishes* Collins 1974

Tait, R. V. *Elements of Marine Ecology* Butterworth 1972. This book deals with all the main processes at work in the sea's living systems around the world.

## SPECIAL BOOKS

*Janes Fighting Ships. Janes Commercial Ships* Janes Publishing Co. (Published at regular intervals). These two volumes are a complete account of all the world's military and commercial shipping.

*Mitchell Beazley Atlas of the Oceans* 1977 (Rand McNally)

*Times Atlas of the Oceans* Times Publishing Co. 1983.

These two atlases are richly illustrated with maps and excellent photographs and diagrams. They also have a wealth of text dealing with every aspect of the oceans.